MORE!

AWESOME JOKES

EVERY VOL 2

9 YEAR OLD SHOULD KNOW!

Design: Fanni Williams / thehappycolourstudio.com
Icons made by: Freepik from www.flaticon.com

www.matwaugh.co.uk

Produced by Big Red Button Books,
a division of Say So Media Ltd.

ISBN: 978-1-912883-13-4

Published: July 2019

A note for parents and readers from the USA: I'm British. I can't help it. I'm a bloke
who goes on holiday for a fortnight, never uses a washroom and comes home knackered.
I don't have a Scooby-Doo who the Red Sox are, or what I should do with a doohickey.
There's only one or two about the Queen (sorry, Ma'am), but you may still find a few that
aren't your cup of tea. The rest? Hopefully they're the bee's knees!

MORE! MORE! MORE!
AWESOME JOKES
EVERY 9 YEAR OLD SHOULD KNOW! VOL 2

MAT WAUGH
ILLUSTRATIONS BY INDREK SILVER EINBERG

Hey – you're back!

I have the memory of a goldfish, but I'm sure we've met somewhere before... did you read the first book of Awesome Jokes? You did?

Wow, haven't you grown!

Doesn't it drive you crackers when adults say that? When you're dragged along to see Great Aunt Nelly and she leans down with her whiffy coffee breath and gives you a hug? Yuck.

There's none of that nonsense here – just a bulging, squirming sack of jokes that I've been raising in my back garden. Expect cheeky ones, shrieky ones, and even a few sneaky ones to make you think!

Ready? It's time to pull out a wriggler, let it go and see who laughs!

‼ This sign means the joke is a super-tough nut to crack. Do you get them all? **‼**

PS Got your own tip-top joke? Get it on the **World Map of Awesome Jokes***! See page 93.*

↓ Laughs start here ↓

Did you hear about the polar explorer who got terrible frostbite in his feet?
He keeps his momentoes on the mantelpiece!

How do you make an egg timer work faster?
Fill it with quicksand!

Which fruit can give you a nasty nip?
A crab apple!

Where does the queen wear her diamond earrings?
On her chandel-ears!

Why was the swotty violinist kicked out of the orchestra?
Because he was always taking notes!

I've swallowed my referee's coin!
And how do you feel now?
I can't decide!

If someone serves you fish and chips, where should you sprinkle the salt?
All over the plaice!

I was asked to give the opening speech at the World Tenpin Bowling Conference.
How did you get on?
Brilliant – I had them rolling in the aisles!

 **My stomach is bloated. Look at it, that's not normal is it? The skin's all stretched, it's taut like a drum.**
OK, OK, no need to bang on about it!

What do you call a clumsy butcher?
Hamfisted!

What do they serve at the annual dinner of the Circle Appreciation Club?
Snacks all round!
(They did try angles, but nobody liked them!)

How are you getting on so far? Is it all making sense? Here's another one for you:

What do you call a silly sentence?
An idiom!

That's not only the world's unfunniest joke, it's the secret to lots of funnies in this book. An idiom is a phrase or sentence that doesn't mean what it says. Work them out – or look them up – and you've got the joke!

I bet you already know hundreds of idioms. Some are **a piece of cake** (easy peasy), others are a bit more **thorny** (tricky)!

If they **drive you crazy** or some jokes in this book **have you stumped**, then **hang in there** – or maybe **sleep on it** and **pick someone's brains** tomorrow!

What do you call a clumsy baker?
Butterfingers!

Who does the Queen call when she wants a trim?
The Royal Hair Force!

How does she say thank you?
She gives them hairmiles!

I asked for directions to the curtain shop but a man sent me up a blind alley instead!

What's a cat's best hand of cards?

All fours!

I've been bitten by a snake!
Hmm. Where were you when it happened?
At the top of a ladder!
Will I be OK?
I'm afraid you're back to square one.

Did you know Cinderella has become a tennis coach?
Now the ball is in her court.

Why should you never give advice to an airline pilot?
Because fly tipping is illegal!

Why was the giraffe keeper sacked?
He said he wouldn't touch them with a ten-foot pole!

JOKES YOUR AUNTIE WON'T LIKE!

Auntie: do you pronounce it *arntie* or *anti*? If it's *arntie*, skip to page 12 because these jokes will make no sense! DON'T SAY I DIDN'T TELL YOU!

Which relative should take a shower?
Anti Bacteria!

What's her sister called?
Anti Fungal!

Which relative has been working out?
Anti Perspirant!

And who's great fun at a party?
Anti Social!

Which relative should you see after a snakebite?
Anti Dote!

And who should you ask if your watch breaks?
Anti Clockwise!

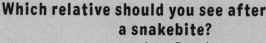

Toasters are great. They're the best invention since sliced bread!

Never ask a hairdryer for advice.
They're always blowing hot and cold.

Did you hear? The town librarian has been fired for stealing.
Wow, really?
I heard they threw the book at her.

That's not all. The chef at the library canteen has lost his job, too.
What for?
They say he was cooking the books.

Why do demolition experts tell the best jokes?
They always bring the house down!

DOCTOR, DOCTOR!

I feel like a battery!
Are you positive?

What do you call a woman who eats omelettes every day?
Highly egg-centric!

How do you encourage a timid rock climber?
Shout 'Boulder!'

Knock Knock!

Who's there?
Isla!
Isla who?
I love you too! Now put your teeth back in.

Teacher: Do you know where the city of Anchorage is?
Student: I don't know, but my gran might.
Alaska.

What was the final score at the World Box Building Championships?
It ended all square.

What about at the World Furniture Making Competition?
Same result – they called it a drawer.

My left leg tingles when it's going to rain!
Ah yes. It looks as if you have a weather vein.

What do you call a vicious insect on the high seas?
Assailant!

What type of sand sticks words together?

Ampersand!

**Why did the sausage and chips go
to the police station?**
They said they'd been battered and assaulted!

Where do windows find love?
On a blind date.

**Why did Cinderella's sisters tell her off
every time the doorbell rang?**
It was the bell of the bawl!

My friend isn't allowed to play with us
any more because he broke the drumkit.
Now he's my secret banned mate.

When the inventor of the pink milkshake died,
what did his friends do at his funeral?
They berried him!

If your baby is the size of a houseboat,
what should you do?
Give it a wide berth.

How do you add firelighters to your
shopping basket online?
Dragon drop!

Why do robots get angry?

Because people are always pushing their buttons!

How do you give an anchor a lift?
Yank his chain!

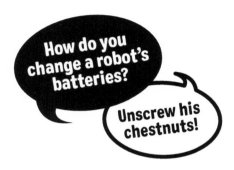

What did the happy robot say to the grumpy robot?
Why do you have a chip on your shoulder?

Did you hear about the criminal comedian?
They clapped him in jail!

Why is Christmas a terrible time to give stuff up?
Because nobody wants to go cold turkey on Christmas Day!

Did you hear about the clown who took a pack of Skittles into his juggling exam?
He passed with flying colours!

Why is it impossible to argue with someone in the desert?
Because you'll always know where they're coming from!

What do you call a fight in the playground after a tricky lesson?
The aftermath!

WHAT'S UP? SUMMIT'S HAPPENING...

What do you call a dictionary on a mountain?
High definition!

What do you call a tent on a mountain?
High pitched!

What do you call it when you kiss and make up on a mountain?
High resolution!

What kind of mountain do ghosts live on?
Highly spirited!

What do you call a clock up a mountain?
High handed!

What do you call a computer up a mountain?
High tech!

What do call a guitar up a mountain?
Highly strung!

What do you call a woman in a dress up a mountain?
High fashion!

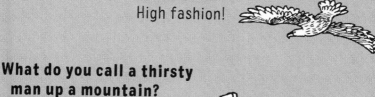

What do you call a thirsty man up a mountain?
High and dry!

What do you call vowels up a mountain?
High five!

My granddad used to be a pirate.
He still wears the eyepatch, just to keep his eye in!

What mouse has no name?

Anony-mouse!

How do you make a couch potato cry?
Give him a bowl of chips.

In a choir of ants, which one always gets the best reception?
The ant-tenor!

What do you call a fruit in trouble?
A damson in distress!

Love anagrams? Here's one for you!

What did the boy do when he found the letters DYNAMO stuck to his fridge?
He decided to make a day of it.

Why wasn't his Mum impressed?
She'd seen better days.

What did the woman do when her boyfriend painted her house black?
She told him never to darken her door again!

Even the ghosts didn't enjoy this year's country fair.
They said it was a fête worse than death!

Why shouldn't you argue with a gardening salsa dancer?
Because she digs in her heels!

Why does Santa carry all the heavy presents?
They could be harmful to his elf!

How do you buy a well online?

Use the drop-down menu!

Why did the hot air balloon crash?

The pilot was having a bad air day!

What did the car fanatic hang above his baby's cradle?
An auto mobile!

Where's the best place to get a massage?
In the back room!

And where would I find it?
Down a back street!

What do you call a ghost that appears in the spring?
An April ghoul!

What's a butcher's favourite boardgame?
Backgammon!

 **I get terrible déjà vu!**
I know, you told me that when you came in yesterday.

What's the difference between drainpipes and bagpipes?
You can always ask your neighbour for help when your drainpipes are blocked!

How does an accountant make her bed?
Using a spreadsheet!

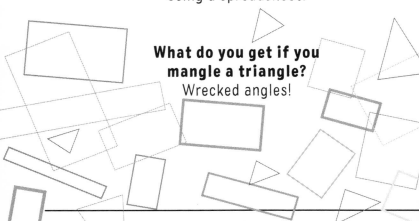

What do you get if you mangle a triangle?
Wrecked angles!

What do you call a launchpad for kittens?
A catapult!

Who's the first to arrive at the theatre?
The prompt!

What do you get if you add...
three volcanoes
two meteorites
one tsunami
and give them all a shake?
A recipe for disaster!

Where's the soggiest place on a llama farm?
Anywhere within spitting distance!

**My son drew a picture of me with no pupils
and the words TUBBY DAD underneath.**
"Is it finished?" he asked me.
I told him to dot the eyes and cross the tease.

**My uncle built a hotel at the top of
a mountain. It used to be great, but now
it's going downhill fast.**

Did you see that new play about onions?
There wasn't a dry eye in the house.

Where do you buy lynx?

At a chain store!

Why do tall people plan for a helicopter ride?

They need to get their ducks in a row!

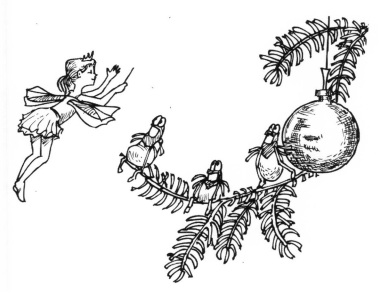

What do ticks sing at Christmas?

Fleas Navidad!

A man walks into a bar. "Get out, I don't like your face!"

It was a crossbar.

PUPPY JOKES AHEAD!

What do call a skydiving puppy?
A parapet!

What do you call a musical puppy?
A trumpet!

What do you call a hairdressing puppy?
A snippet!

What do you call a puppy that makes a mess?
A crumpet!

What do you call a puppy on a hot day?
A limpet!

What do you call a puppy who does what he's told?
A puppet!

DOCTOR, DOCTOR!

My mum wanted to give me alphabet spaghetti because she said I liked it.
I told her not to put words into my mouth.

My aunt has a head shaped like a triangle.
They say she has a great ear for music.

Why are vampires selfish at sport?
Because they always go into bat first!

My neighbour doesn't stop talking.
When we're both in the garden she won't let me get a word in hedgeways!

My friend said she could make an omelette without using her hands.
She soon ended up with egg on her face!

I'm sure that one of my teachers has cast a spell on me.
Which one?
Yes, you're probably right!

What hurts more than being hit by a falling lampshade?
Candle whacks!

Who's there?
Curf!
Curf who?
Curfew just started, now let me in!

What does a new emperor do after breakfast?
Wipes Greece off the map!

Where do you find the eye of the storm?
In the middle of hurr cane!

DOCTOR, DOCTOR!

A fortune teller told me I'd die if anyone interrupted –
Oh do pull yourself together, you can't believe that nonsense.
THUD!
Whoops! Looks like I spoke too soon.

What was Henry VIII's motto?
Chop and Change!

Why should you never go climbing in a tomb with a numb thumb?
Because of all the silent bees!

What do you call a tree that travels at 50mph?
A beech buggy!

 **There's a man in your waiting room who can multiply 438 x 43362 in his head!**
I've told you before, don't test my patients!

My brother always skips my favourite song half way through.
If he does it again I'm telling Dad, but then I'll never hear the end of it!

Did you hear about the man who left his job in the shoelace factory?
He couldn't make ends meet.

(Think that was bad? How about this one!)
Did you hear about the butcher who gave up making sausages?
He couldn't make both ends meat!

What do you call a photographer who has fallen asleep in his vegetable patch?
A *landscape* gardener!

LOOKING FOR COW JOKES?

What do you call a cow that creeps up on you and shouts MOO!?
Unforsee-a-bull!

What do you call a cow that's been buried?
Biodegrade-a-bull!

What do you call a lazy cow?
Unemploy-a-bull!

What do you call a superhero cow?
Incredibly cape-a-bull!

What do you call a cow that won't stand still?
Immeasur-a-bull!

What do you call an invisible cow?
Undetect-a-bull!

What do you call a cow in a small space?
Compress-i-bull!

What do you call a cow that always wins at conkers?
Unconquer-a-bull!

What do you call a cow that tramples all over your vegetable patch?
Unforgive-a-bull!

How did the dad describe his decision to get a cow for a pet?
Regret-a-bull!

...and what is his advice to other dads?
Forget-a-bull!

What animal comes before seagull in the dictionary?
A beagle!

Why do herb gardeners always make a mess?
Because thyme flies when you're having fun!

Who's there?
Eileen!
Eileen who?
Eileen on your doorbell, but it doesn't work!

**My granny was an inventor.
She tried building a spaghetti
airplane, but it never took off.**

Then she made one out of chocolate,
but my grandad said she should keep
her feat on the ground.

What's the best button on a baker's oven?
Automatic Pie - Lots!

 **My hamster died last year and I haven't stopped crying.**
Good grief!

How will you keep warm on the trip to the North Pole?
I'll wear a hat and alpaca jumper!

Why don't silly people get earworms?
Because they go in one ear and out the other!

You must be joking!

Humph... this section makes me grumpy. Since Book 1, nine year olds from around the world have been sending me their jokes. I wouldn't mind because I love getting emails. But the problem is... THEY'RE FUNNY.

This is not how it's supposed to work. Grown-ups know best. Grown-ups *are* the best. Just leave the funnies to me, OK? 😠

DANIEL FROM CAMBRIDGE, ENGLAND

I am green, I can be served, but not eaten. What am I?

A tennis ball!

JUDAH FROM ISRAEL

Why do people always leave their cardigan in their car?

Because it's a CARdigan!

What did one snowman say to the other snowman?

Can you smell carrot?

What is a chicken's favourite weapon?

What did the frog say when he ate too many flies?

The eggs-terminator!

Ouch, my stomach is BUGGING me!

What is a pensioner's favourite drink?

Elderflower!

Why are French cats so LOUD?

Because they like to *chat*!
Don't get it? Ask a French speaker!

Where does a soldier keep his armies?

In his sleevies!

Knock, Knock!
Who's there?
Burglar.
Burglar who?
Burglars don't knock!

Do you have a great joke? Get it on the **World Map of Awesome Jokes** – see page 93!

Why can't bridges concentrate at school?
They have very short attention spans!

My Auntie doesn't take her dog Avie out during the summer. Why not?
Avie-ate-her sunglasses!

How did the hot air balloon pilot learn the secret of the cows?
He over herd it!

What is the medical name for counting sheep?
Woolly thinking!

When did European people wear bad jumpers and listen to terrible music?
In the Middle Ages!

You might need to ask someone old about this one!

Knock Knock!
Who's there?
Despair!
Despair who?
Despair is rotten, can I have an apple instead please?

Why didn't the bear get the job?
He didn't have the koala-fications!

Why should bears and penguins never meet?
They're polar opposites!

What do you call a wig for a grizzly?
A trans-fur!

Waiter, Waiter!

Why have you taken my girlfriend's lunch away?
'Caesar salad,' you said.
So I did, sir!

I saw a really boring TV show about paint drying last night.
That's nothing – I saw a fly-on-the-wall documentary!

How do you find a woman who smells of sausages?
With a sniff-her dog!

I tried to insulate my loft with straw and cotton. I even tried wool.
Did it help?
No... in the end the roo-fur did it!

Knock Knock! — **Who's there?**
Marmoset!
Marmoset who?
Marmoset I had to be home by six o'clock!

Why should a solar eclipse be made illegal?
It's daylight robbery!

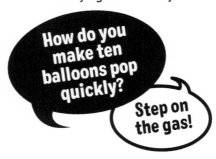

How do you make ten balloons pop quickly?

Step on the gas!

**Why did the manager get sacked from his job
at the ball bearing factory?**
He couldn't keep on top of all the orders!

**What happened when the wig-maker
crashed his car?**
The hairbags went off!

Waiter,
Waiter!

**This crispy duck tastes
horrible! I won't pay for it!**
I'm so sorry, sir. I'll de-ducked it
immediately.

What do you call a man who wears a suit of armour in a tornado?
A knightingale!

Why shouldn't you wear a suit of armour to bed?
It'll give you knight-mares!

How often did the king attack the castle?
Fort-knightly!

How do you hide a man called Arthur?
With an over-knight bag!

Why does a knight need an iPhone?
To check his chain mail!

Did you hear about the umbrella that fell over and killed a man in a suit of armour?
It was a deadly knight-shade!

What did St George wear to the party?
A knight-dress!

What did St George call his moody horse?
A knight-mare!

DOCTOR, DOCTOR! I'm addicted to snooker! How can you help me?
Give me a break!

Did you hear about the hikers on the remote forest path?
Their plans went bear-shaped!

3 TEA JOKES: TAKE 'EM OR LEAF 'EM!

What type of tea do cave divers like?
Cavity!

What type of tea do clowns like?
Jollity!

What type of tea do naked people like?
Nudity!

What do you call a bee that can't get into the party?
A wanna-bee!

How do you remove a hair that's stuck in your mouth?

Use a fine tooth comb!

What's the difference between hive and aisle?
Hive forgotten, but aisle probably remember soon!

My dog got lost in the fog.
How did he look when you found him?
Mistified!

If your walls are made of paper, what do you need?
Light switches!

I went to a honey exhibition last week.
Was it good?
**Yes, they were giving away loads
of free-bees!**

**Knock
Knock!**

Who's there?
Cedar!
Cedar who?
Cedar sun? It's going down,
now let me in.

**Did you hear about the man who fell and broke his
arm on his way to the bathroom?**
It was a hard landing!

How does a blue whale connect to the internet?
Using Bluetooth!

**My gym teacher has been teaching us how
to do the plank for an hour.**
How do you feel now?
Board stiff!

FOUR SHARP HEDGEHOG JOKES!

What do you call a hedgehog shop?
Selling point!

What do you call an escaping hedgehog?
Vanishing point!

What do you call a hedgehog's best friend?
Beside the point!

What do you call a hedgehog that's one in a hundred?
Percentage point!

DOCTOR, DOCTOR! ➕

My vision is blurred and I keep getting headaches.
I suggest you visit BlindfoldsForSale.com
Will it help?
Oh yes. It's a site for sore eyes!

What do you call a dodgy fishmonger?
An eeler-dealer!

What's the best way to abduct a seabird?
Take terns!

Knock Knock!

Who's there?
Oil spill!
Oil spill who?
Oil spill my drink if you open
the door suddenly!

This pie is mouldy! You should sack your chef!
Oh I did, sir, last week. He made the pie before he left.

Which clock has hands and a face, goes quicker at weekends and runs on baked beans?
Your body clock!

When I'm in the garden, how do I know that my lunch is ready?
My crow waves!

What do you call a bird that follows you around online?
A cyber storker!

I made a cake but I accidentally baked the scales as well. Will I be OK?
Oh yes, I always recommend a balanced diet!

What do you call a snail with a library on its back?
Shelf-ish!

What kind of dive is sticky, dark and dangerous?
A nosedive!

Why couldn't the barber find a girlfriend?
He always cut his dates short!

What did the gym teacher say when he saw the boy with springs on his feet?
That boy is definitely for the high jump!

My cousin has a lettuce leaf sticking out of his ear.
Why don't doctors pull it out?
They think it's the just the tip of the iceberg!

Why don't roofers make any money?

Because everything they do is on the house!

Waiter, Waiter!

I wanted this to be a meal to remember, but there's no topping on this pizza!
Give me your camera, sir, and say cheese!

This steak is tiny!
I'm sorry, sir, the chef is trying out some new short cuts.

Why is it impossible to stay grumpy in a soft play centre?
Because there's no hard feelings!

How do you put up Lost Kitten signs?
Cat and paste!

Why does my wife hit the roof whenever I'm behind the wheel?
It sounds like you're driving her up the wall!

Who's there?
Tamara!
Tamara who?
Tamara is nearly here, now let me in!

**What do you call a man who worships
fried potatoes?**
A chipmonk!

**I can't stop giving
chocolate to cows.**
Don't worry, that's
treat-a-bull!

What did the boy with gold up his nose discover?
Rich pickings!

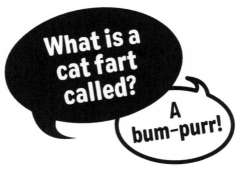

What is a cat fart called?

A bum-purr!

What's the least reliable part of a jam tart?
The flaky pastry!

How did the criminal try to avoid the speeding fine?
By lying low!

Why was the farmer's herd smaller than he thought?
He'd mis-cow-nted!

Did you see the sheep-shaped sheikh seek shade?

How does mummy crab get her babies to bed?
With a nip and a tuck!

What do you call a child who refuses to sleep in a big bed?
A boycott!

What do you call lightning at night?

A flash black!

What do you call a woman who comes home after spending too much at the jewellery store?
Mum-bling!

 **Why is there a mattress on the road underneath your office window?**
That's because you and I are about to fall OUUUUUUUUUUUUUUT!

What do you call a bottom made of wood?
A beech bum!

I've heard you have the best wine in town. Is that true?
Absolutely. You, sir, are an overfed buffoon with more money than sense. I despise you even more than I hate my terrible job.
You're so rude!
You're welcome. Do let me know if you'd like some more whine.

What do you call ancestors from Poland?
Been Poles!

How does an astronomers' birthday party start?
With a Big Bang!

Why should sailors beware when sailing from the Atlantic to the Pacific?
Because of the different current-seas!

Why did the man wearing an elephant outfit run out of money
Because everywhere he went he paid through the nose!

Do you have a cheese grater?
I'm sorry sir, it's the biggest piece we have!

When do children learn to swim?
In their infant-sea!

Why don't crabs fall over?
Because they're so shore-footed!

Why have you prescribed me fuel and a packet of mints?
I'm putting you on the road to recovery!

Why did the man confess?
The police gave him the hard cell!

Knock Knock!
Who's there?
Bustle!
Bustle who?
Bus'll be here in a minute and I've forgotten my homework!

How do butchers end their day?
With a sweep steak!

What's two things should you never pass at the dinner table?
Water and wind!

Every time I open the front door, I get a painful splinter.
Here, use this sandpaper. That should take the edge off it.

Why did the fishmonger lose her job?
She wouldn't move a mussel!

Why do argumentative people never take milk in their coffee?
Because they always answer black!

I've burned my mouth on your boiling hot soup!
I suggest you simmer down, sir!

My uncle is called **Bartholemew Alexander Cornelius Fotherington-Smythe, but he calls himself Bart and hangs out with celebrities.**
What do you call him?
A massive name-dropper!

Who helps people to eat TV dinners?
Tray-knees!

What should you keep your jokes in?
A punnet!

Why couldn't the conductor hear the music?
There was something wrong with his broad band!

Which musical instrument should you take to a desert island?
Castanets!

I got a letter today. The postman bowed as he gave it to me, and told me I looked great. It must have been sent by first class male.

These are very tricky to work out!
How many can you get?

What do you call a girl with a glass of salty water?
Briony!

**What do you call a boy that only knows
four vowels?**
Noah!

**What do you call a boy with a
head like a bridge?**
Archie!

**What do you call a boy that fits
in his mum's pocket?**
Joey!

**What do you do if someone
beats you in a race?**
Get Ethan!
Ethan who?
Ethan Stevens!

Who should you ask to take you across the river?
Roman!

What do you call a man that can make a dog answer the front door?
Patrick!

What do you call a boy that takes your dominos?
Dominic!

What do call a man who used to have black hair?
Grayson!

What do you call a girl with a waterfront pad?
Lily!

What do you call a boy squashed under a cow?
Preston!

What do you call a man in shades?
Hugh!

Why can't you wash a model of the Titanic?

It's un-sink-able!

Did you hear about the man who was arrested for stealing dominoes?
The police caught him in a spot check!

How do you know when tightrope walkers are in love?
When they're going steady!

How do you cross an ocean without getting wet?
Use a walkwave!

My Mum always gives me sandwiches for lunch.
How do you feel?
Bread bored!

Why do bees become managers?
Because they know all the buzzwords!

Why did the dog rip up the script?
It was just a ruff draft!

What do you call a tall attention-seeker?
A pain in the neck!

**Why don't naughty children
get vegetables?**
Because there's no peas for the wicked!

How did the walrus win the talent contest?
With a seal of approval!

My grandad ran the town library until the day he passed away.
How awful! What happened?
He was buried in a book!

Have you heard about the assassin who kills his victims by breaking wind?
They're calling him Silent Butt Deadly!

Why did the golfer get sunburn?
He'd forgotten his handy cap!

How do you find your way inside the Arctic Circle?
Use a floe chart!

What do you call an optician who's hoping to make a lot of money?
Spec-u-later!

How much do dead batteries cost?
Nothing - they're free of charge!

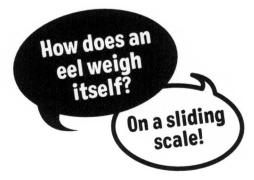

How does an eel weigh itself?

On a sliding scale!

What do you call a bull elephant in a restaurant?
The head weighter!

Did you hear about the judge who liked fishing?
He gave everyone the benefit of the trout.

My Dad eats candles, torches and lamps. Why?
I don't know – he's always been a light eater!

What do carpenters do when they meet?
Swap pleasant-trees!

What do you call a sting that doesn't go away?
Everlast-sting!

Why do fish so bad at playing the guitar?
Because you can tune a guitar, but you can't tuna fish!

What do you call a man who's no good at camping?
Incompe-tent!

 **How do you fix a loose monkey bar?**
Tighten the monkey nut!

**What does a judge say when she enters
a hotel room?**
I rest my case!

What feeling do sheep get in the spring?
Shear delight!

Why do leopards avoid the police?
They're afraid of spot checks!

What do examiners in Beijing play in their spare time?
Chinese checkers!

How do owls take photos?

Point and hoot!

Did you hear about the strongman who could beat a carthorse?
He always pulls a big crowd!

How does a guidedog take a day off work?
He throws a stickie!

What do workers at a lemonade factory wear?
High-fizz jackets!

Why do hedgehogs make the best boxers?
Because they always win on points!

Why couldn't the soccer player find his mail?
Somebody had moved the goalpost!

How do you know when a tailor is coming for Christmas?
He makes his presents felt!

Why did Leonardo da Vinci have so much cutlery?
He was a top drawer!

How do weightlifters give directions?
PowerPoint!

What do you call a fight in the panda enclosure?
Pandamonium!

My Dad was overweight so they put him on a superfast diet. He can eat as much soup as he likes, but he's not allowed to use a spoon.
Wow, what's it called?
Forked lightening!

How do you go to church in the Arctic?

Pray it cool!

When should prisoners be released?
When they pass their cell-by date!

 **How does a boxer do her paperwork?**
With a whole punch!

Why was the singer locked out?
He'd forgotten about the key change!

Did you hear about the farmer who disagreed with the vet's report?
She was mad when she read about the cows, but you should see her now – she's on the ram-page!

Why did the man pack a rod and net for his flight?
He wanted to try fly fishing!

Where do sheep go to chat?

A whine baa!

What do you call a grandmother who mixes up her letters?
An amagran!

Did you hear about the omelette café?
It's closed for a whisk assessment!

I went off cheese for a while... but now I'm feeling feta.

How do vampires gamble?

With high stakes!

When is a funny painting like a vegetable?
When it's an arty-joke!

How do you make an eclair shaped like a train?

With choux pastry!

This is one for all you brilliant spellers out there!

How do you keep track of a baby swan?
Use a signet ring!

Why are sports people ready for their gran to visit?
Because they always try to keep a clean sheet!

My window cleaner refuses to wash the basement windows.
He says he has a very low pane threshold!

How does a mountaineer like his schoolbooks?
Ink-lined!

I almost didn't put this one in because it's so tricky!

What's the best way to see the letters B, R and D?
Take a bird's i view!

What do you call an airbase for pilots on a diet?
A No-Fry Zone!

What do you call two grannies walking in the same direction?
Parallelograns!

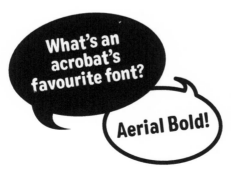

What's an acrobat's favourite font?

Aerial Bold!

Water, sand, ice... can you think of any more?
What are you doing?
My teacher told me to make a bucket list!

What's the best way to write jokes on the beach?

Use Comic Sands!

Why did the hen get two bags of corn in the mail instead of one?
She must have double clucked!

Did you hear about the actor who kept stealing other people's lines?
She was caught in the act!

Why did Aladdin teach his dog to drive?
He'd always wanted a magic car pet!

Why did the kettle whistle out of tune?
Because it needed descaling!

 **Why was Jack arrested?**
For beanstalking!

Why do whales make ruthless soldiers?
They always go in for the krill!

Why are plays about origami so good?
Because you can watch the drama unfold!

My American friends tell me this joke sucks!

My head is a gobstopper, my body is a toffee and my legs are strawberry laces. What am I?
A three-piece sweet!

What does an English golfer carry in her pocket?
A tee bag!

And what are the signs of a forgetful English golfer?
Tee leaves!

What's the easiest way to count a flock of birds?
Add up all the legs and divide by two!

How do you describe a birthday when you don't know what you're going to get?
In the present tense!

A man was sacked after he didn't turn up on the second day and called in sick on the fourth.
He said later that he only does odd jobs.

This next joke is for punctuation fans only!

Did you hear about the child-eating jellyfish?
A boy swapped the hyphen for a space and had the jellyfish for lunch!

When would you need luggage made of paper?
In a worst case scenario!

**Did you hear about the man who was
thrown out of the coffee shop?**
Staff reported that he had an axe to grind!

**A man who left without paying for his coffee has
been caught on camera.**
Police say they have some excellent mug shots.

**What do you call a broken pencil you
can't take back to the shop?**
The point of no return!

**How do you write 'percussion
instrument' in emojii?**
With a pair of symbols!

If a man aged 47 eats toast, what does he put on?
Middle-aged spread!

**How do you get past a graveyard of vampires
with just a pair of scissors?**
Quickly cut across!

**Why are caterpillar thieves never given a
fair chance?**
Because every time they turn over a new leaf
they get sent back to prison!

Where do saints who can't spell go when they die?
To live in heaven, surrounded by angles!

Now it's your turn!

Writing jokes is simple, isn't it? You just think of something funny!

But that's where it gets a bit tricky, because people laugh at different things. You know when you say something hilarious and people look like you've just made a horrible smell? That's what I'm talking about!!

But don't worry – if you make up a joke that gets *most* people chuckling, you've got a good one.

So then: would you like the chance to show the world how screamingly funny you are? Let's go!

If you already have a humdinger, then read on. But if you fancy writing your own, and you like drawing too, then get your thinking cap on and your pencils ready, and turn to page 94!

I know a great joke!

If you're sitting on a zinger, there are two possibilities:

1 - your bottom is a bit itchy
2 - you already have a brilliant, clever and super funny joke.

If it's number 1, I recommend that you see a doctor, pronto.

If it's number 2, then send your joke to me and I'll put it on my **World Map of Awesome Jokes**!

Head over to the map now to discover silly jokes, clever jokes and weird jokes. Some jokes rhyme, some are a crime, but they're all sent in by children like you!

Could you be the first on the map from your town?

et a grown-up to send in your joke:
ww.matwaugh.co.uk/jokemap

Jokers wanted!

Could you write and illustrate your own joke?

There are lots of different types of jokes. Many jokes use *surprise*. Think about this classic (not one of mine!):

> **What's brown and sticky?**

The first time you heard this you were probably thinking of all the brown, sticky and smelly things in the world! But here comes the answer:

> **A stick!**

Surprise! It's not rude at all, and now you're thinking about how you've been tricked by two meanings of the word 'sticky'. It's a very clever joke.

So let's try something easier: a pun. Puns are great fun for kids because the sillier they are, the better! Here's how it works. Start with a great word: **humbug**. In Britain, a humbug is a type of hard, minty sweet or candy (yummy). But what does humbug *sound* like? It sounds like a joke!

> **What do you call an insect that doesn't know the words?**
> A humbug!

That's just the start. Find humbug rhymes – even if they're not real words – and you can make lots *more* jokes!

How? Just go through the alphabet letter by letter, changing the first sound (ignore the vowels: a, e, i, o & u).
- Don't forget that some sounds are made up of more than one letter, like *cr-*, *ch-* and *th-*.
- If you're feeling adventurous, you can use 'nearly' rhymes, too. As long as the word sounds similar, it's good!

Let's try it out with **(h)**umbug:

b) → *b*umbug. Oops, what a way to start: I made a rude word! I won't use that one or I'll be in trouble!

c) → *c*omebug. That's good! Let me think...

> **What do you call an obedient insect?**
> A comebug!

Not bad, but I bet you can do better! What about *chumbug*, or *crumbug*? *Dumbug*? It's your turn!

How did you get on? Have you invented a brand new bug joke?

Great! Now every awesome joke needs a fantastic illustration, just like the ones in this book by super-clever Indrek. He's really thought about the jokes, and added lots of extra detail to make them even funnier.

So now you can do the same. Use the page opposite to tell and draw your bug joke, and don't forget to make that picture really funny!

If you'd like a bigger sheet to draw on, you can download one to print out at *matwaugh.co.uk/wall*

Happy? Ask a grown-up to take a picture and send it to jokes@matwaugh.co.uk – I'll put all the best ones on the **Wall Of Awesome Jokes** on my website.

Happy bug hunting!

Parents: see the website for full terms and conditions.

My Awesome Joke!

Question: _____
_____
_____

Answer: _____

My illustration:

first name: _____ Age: _____

me town and country: _____

Did you know that the first
microscopes were called
flea glasses!

Phew, we're done!

Reviews of joke books are almost as funny as the books themselves.

You're not funny!
These jokes are too old!
These jokes are for babies!
These jokes are too rude!

I get all of those and I don't mind: it just shows that everyone is different! But if you have something nice to say about this book, or you're just really funny – then please pop over to Amazon with your parent and write something about this book so others know what to expect.

As long as you found something to laugh about, I'm happy too!

About Mat Waugh

In the first book, I told you about my batty aunt. Here are some new things about me.

I have big crow's feet. I know what you're thinking – how do I buy my shoes? But crow's feet are those wrinkles that grown-ups get next to their eyes.

Some people get crow's feet because they need glasses but don't wear them enough (true).

Some people get them because their skin doesn't have enough oil, called sebum. I only included this fact because then I can write the word *see-bum*. (What?! That's how you say it!).

But I get crow's feet because I spend a lot of time squinting at my three children, trying to give them Paddington hard stares. They ignore me.

I've jumped out of a plane, done bungee jumps and tried wreck diving. I even met Mrs Waugh at a theme park. But last week I got dizzy on the trampoline. The lesson? **Never get old, children!**

I still can't do handstands. I'm practising.

I produce enough dribble each day to fill a water bottle, and enough each year to fill the bath.*

My favourite sounds are birdsong, tapping keys, and windmills.

When I was 19 I had a ticket for a flight with some friends, but there wasn't enough space. The airline put us on a tiny plane instead and I sat in the co-pilot's seat. While my friends were sleeping in the back, the pilot let me have a go at flying the plane.

I've taken a photo of my daughters every single Sunday since they were born. I'm very proud of this, as I'm not very good at homework. In nearly every photo, they're pulling a silly face at me.

Finally, I love getting emails (but ask your parents first!). You can reach me here: mail@matwaugh.co.uk

* So do you!

Three more to try!

Cheeky Charlie series
Meet Harriet and her small, stinky brother. Together, they're trouble. Fabulously funny stories that will keep you snorting way past bedtime.

Fantastic Wordsearches
Wordsearch with a difference: themed, crossword clues and hidden words await!

The Fun Factor
When the fun starts vanishing from Thora's village, she's the only one to notice. Frosty the headmaster is definitely up to no good, but what about Dad's new girlfriend? A mystery adventure story for gadget-loving kids aged 8+.

Available from Amazon and local bookshops.

Be the first to know about new stuff! Sign up for my emails at matwaugh.co.uk

Made in the USA
Las Vegas, NV
12 February 2023

67361619R00062